Explore the secrets of seasonal colour analysis

Seasonal colour analysis has been [barcode obscures text] the rich and famous for far too long, [obscured] back home to all of us! Its not [obscured] making of a magazine [obscured] ard to sharing some valuable [obscured]

Since Stylemine my personal service began several years ago my goal was to make colour analysis accessible bringing it to where it could be of use to people from Christmas markets fashion events and more. Many people were curious about it but may not have otherwise endeavored to seek out about this truly life enhancing practical formula that once mastered alters shopping habits for the better forever!

The science supporting the finding of your very own seasonal colour code is transformative and outlined in detail within this handbook. Once learnt it really changed my outlook, I wouldn't have enthusiasm about anything that didn't inspire me as I've always been skeptical of many things until I saw the results for myself.

While I will go into detail regarding the methodology of Colour analysis that I was taught in the first two chapters, the whole purpose for each of us after this is to take the ball and run with it. Developing an eye for the seasonal harmony is something that we should seek, we can all do this.
I will give you some tips that I've leant from styling clients and being an artist that will help.

When I paint a portrait, I look for harmony and discord only when it really works is the portrait is complete and representing the desired feeling. Colours are a powerful tool of everyday armory they can literally give us their energy.

In a world more and more about image and artificial ones at that, we should never neglect our substance, nature would never do that even though the consumer world can. If we use natures gift of seasonal harmony in our wardrobe we can like that portrait literally resonate with our own natural essence!

Knowing your colours can also save you from making those regrettable purchases, you can instead scan the through rows of hangers knowing with confidence what clothing will suit you best. It will free up your wardrobe for the items that will make your image really work. You will find it saves time and money you won't look at colours and clothing in the same way again!

I wanted to create a handbook that would help my clients to help themselves. Too many professions make themselves the sole keeper of knowledge so that clients form a dependency, whereas my aim is to give you back in a way that empowers something that you probably already have an instinct for but with a little help it can be heightened so that you have your own eureka moment! From there you can go in leaps and bounds towards what we all aim for, the feeling of confidence in ourselves, the choices we make and the things that we attract into our lives.

For many people shopping at various times in life can be a minefield, for those with little time to shop or seeking a total image revamp I can still offer personal shopping trips, wardrobe detoxes or personal styling advice online. I can wrap around many different styling services to offer you a personal answer to any dilemmas faced. For more information just go to my website www.stylemine.co.uk

I hope you are ready to find lots of inspiring tips in the Stylemine Handbook, no more digging around as if mining for something in the dark, turn on those lights and be prepared to find treasure or maybe even dynamite!

Chapter 1 – The Feeling of Colour   page 4

Chapter 2 – The technique of season finding   page 6

Chapter 3 – Spring Summer Winter Spring   page 11

Chapter 4 – Muted and Vivid Warm and Cool   page 19

Chapter 5 – How to develop an eye for colour   page 21

Chapter 6 – Shopping tips   page 22

Chapter 7 – Previous Clients   page 26

The Feeling of Colour

To feel the power of colour a little defocusing is needed, the first aspect we identify in both the season, and the client, is either a warm or a cool tone and that is very much about feeling not just prescriptive.

Warm colours can be any colour at all other than white or black, the factor we look for is the temperature. The warmer blues and greens have vivid qualities which would be prevalent if we picture a bright spring day full of flowers new grass and spring light. The Autumn season is also warm but will have darker or more muted qualities in similar blues and greens.

Does the colour make you feel warm or cold as that is a good indication of temperature and season, it's the first step towards the very tip of the iceberg on a journey to unearthing the power within colours!

Greens of Summer can be sage like, cool often like a faded sunbaked field through hazy sunshine, a similar muted quality to Autumn although Autumn has a richer smoky fire aspect to it.

Blues of summer are like those endless summer days in the late afternoon. Unlike the other cool season Winter that replicates some of these colours but with more intensity, where deep fir tree leaves contrast with a less blended scene of crisp blue sky without haze or teal blur of any kind.

So warm and cool are a feeling and then when we learn more it becomes a seasonal feeling –

Warm - Spring and Autumn are warm, spring clearer Autumn less so.

Cool - Summer and Winter are cool, where Winter is clear and sharp summer is less so. The colour wheel shows how the cool and warm and the vivid and muted connect with one another.

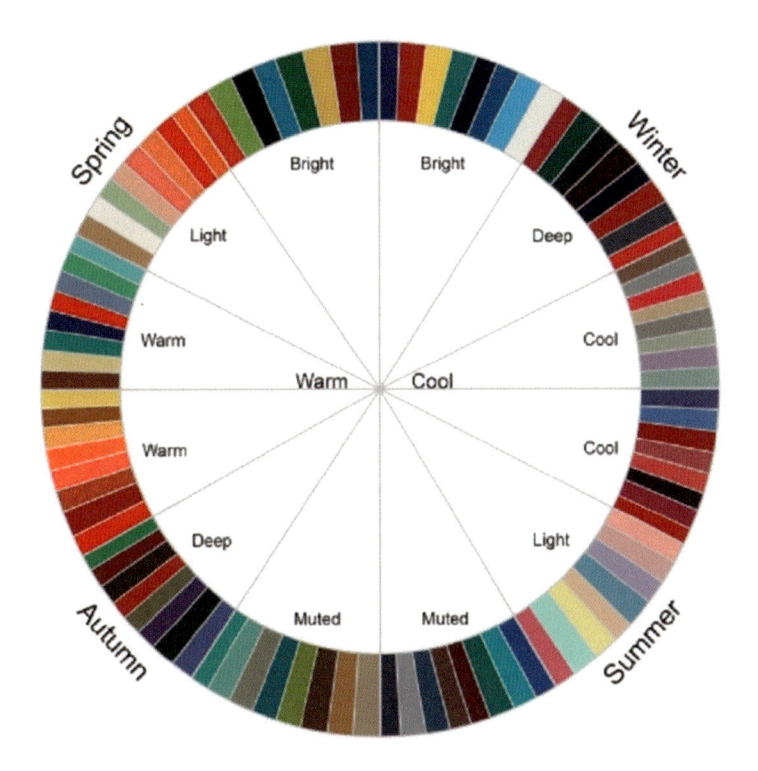

The technique of season finding

Once we become familiar with the characteristics of seasons being warm or cool, and then vivid or more sublime and muted we can go on to understand how to apply that principle to finding a seasonal harmony in ourselves and others, that is where the magic begins!

How colour is received by others

Red – Its powerful and quickly perceived as it activates the pituitary gland raising heartrates, dynamic and attention grabbing true red can be worn by any of the seasons. The hot vivid and salmon pink variant is also vital youthful and lively it is best celebrated by those in the spring season.

Pink – Soft pink or soft lilac is always delicate and romantic, it is lovely on a person with Summers seasonal colouring, although if a little peachier it suits spring very well or the lilac has some extra vibrancy. The bright pink and magenta are great for a flash of brilliance against the tones of winter colouring. Autumns wear salmon pink well and if it gravitates to a duskier deeper shade all the better.

Purple – Purple power has the creativity edge, when worn it conveys mystery spirituality even royalty. Spring has vital warm violet hues both light or dark. Summer cool indigos either pastel or with a medium strong pigmentation.

Blue – Has a reputation of conveying dependability responsibility and trust. The smoky blues of Summer are a more light-hearted version, but they can also include navy and far darker blues as can all the seasons to fully embody this effect. Springs blues are often turquoise and lively, autumns are similar but far deeper and less vivid.

Green – Green implies relaxation and a oneness with nature. Summers are soft, spring greens are the brightest, Autumn greens are very earthy, while deeper greens are associated with wealth and prestige suiting Winter colouring perfectly.

Yellow – Yellow is the colour to communicate optimism and warmth, it has ochre shades in Autumn that merge with brighter almost lime shades in spring. Summer has cool oatmeal faded corn colours and soft sunlight, it can also work in Winter if its intense and less warm.

There's a lot more to understand but now the seasonal colours have more meaning, and it will all come together in technicolour as you read on and practice looking at the colour charts and images further on.

 Now's the time to add people to this knowledge! The harmony continues, going hand in hand with the colours within our skin eyes and hair. The under current of the colour of the skin is what matters here, it shines from beneath the surface and is key to the proper evaluation of tone and warmth. It is quite different from just looking superficially at pigmentation. Someone with a very dark skin tone can be of cool colouring. It is the warm colours in the colour charts below that will be less present and determine the season as cool, the undertones will be the glow from beneath the saturation of colour. Equally spring and autumn toned people can appear fair or dark but the warm under glow will confirm it.

So now we look at ourselves or our friends and family, makeup free in natural lighting -

SPRING WARM LIGHT BRIGHT

Hair Colour – golden brown, golden blonde, strawberry blond, strawberry red, auburn, red, black brown, golden grey.

Skin Colour – peach, rosy cheeks, golden beige, ivory, ivory with golden brown freckles.

Eye Colour – clear blue, clear green, turquoise, bright blue, light golden brown.

AUTUMN WARM SOFT DEEP

Hair Colour – red, copper, light red brown, golden brown, chestnut, dark red brown, charcoal black, golden grey, charcoal brown.

Skin Colour – dark coppery beige, ivory with golden freckles, golden beige, sallow, peach with golden brown freckles, black with golden undertone.

Eye Colour – golden brown, dark brown, amber, hazel, green with brown and gold flecks, pale clear green, blue with turquoise.

SUMMER - SOFT COOL LIGHT

Hair Colour – ash blonde, platinum blonde, blonde brown, brown grey, brown with a little auburn, blue grey, light brown.

Skin Colour – beige lily with pink cheeks, beige lily no colour, pink beige, peaches and cream,

Eye Colour – cloudy grey, pale grey green, pale grey, green with white flecks, blue with white flecks, hazel, bright clear blue and turquoise, soft brown.

WINTER COOL DEEP BRIGHT

Hair Colour – blue black, medium brown reddish brown, dark brown grey beige tone, salt and pepper, white blonde, silver white.

Skin Colour – lily white, white with pink undertones, beige, rose beige, olive, black with a blue undertone.

Eye Colour – dark reddish brown, hazel, grey blue, blue with white flecks, dark blue, grey green, green with white flecks.

Next, I will depict the seasons with a paint palate of colours and paper dolls. I used the dolls to make a visual impact that can be hung in your wardrobe because as many seasonal colour reminders that you can have around the home or in your handbag the better they will help you to absorb the seasonal range and it will soon become effortless to see the best combinations that are possible.

You will notice very quickly the feel of them, the way each season springs to life in a certain way. I will show how we are the same, we spring to life in individual ways too, and by harnessing the power of our season we can celebrate our own intrinsic image and being.

The seasons colours have a real zing in Spring often people who fit well into the spring season have warm brightness to their features, Goldie Hawn and Tyra Banks are spring as is Nicole Kidman. Springs have eyes that pop often with intense warm blues!

Summers are so cool imagine wearing all those soft colours. Kate Windsor is a good example of summer although the range can include some very pale ashy or golden blondes such as Gwyneth Paltrow and Kate Moss.

Autumn is just divine to see glowing from the following page or being worn by the right person with warm muted features. Teri Hatcher is deep Autumn, Julia Roberts is warm Autumn.

Winter has a real vibrancy that makes me think of clothes worn in the snow, it also contains some surprising mushroom and coffee colours that come alive with a winter person who has cool contrasting features. Rachel Weisz and Lucy Liu are deep winter. They can become strikingly attractive when matched with their correct seasonal clothing

Try holding some of the seasonal colours below your face and check for a harmonizing effect, do they make you healthy and rested? Do they reduce dark circles and bring out your eyes?

Enjoy visualizing the seasons with some of the following images. They teach about what catches the eye seasonally, so becoming a natural eye-catching element of nature can become a habit!

SPRING SUMMER WINTER AUTUMN

SPRING

11

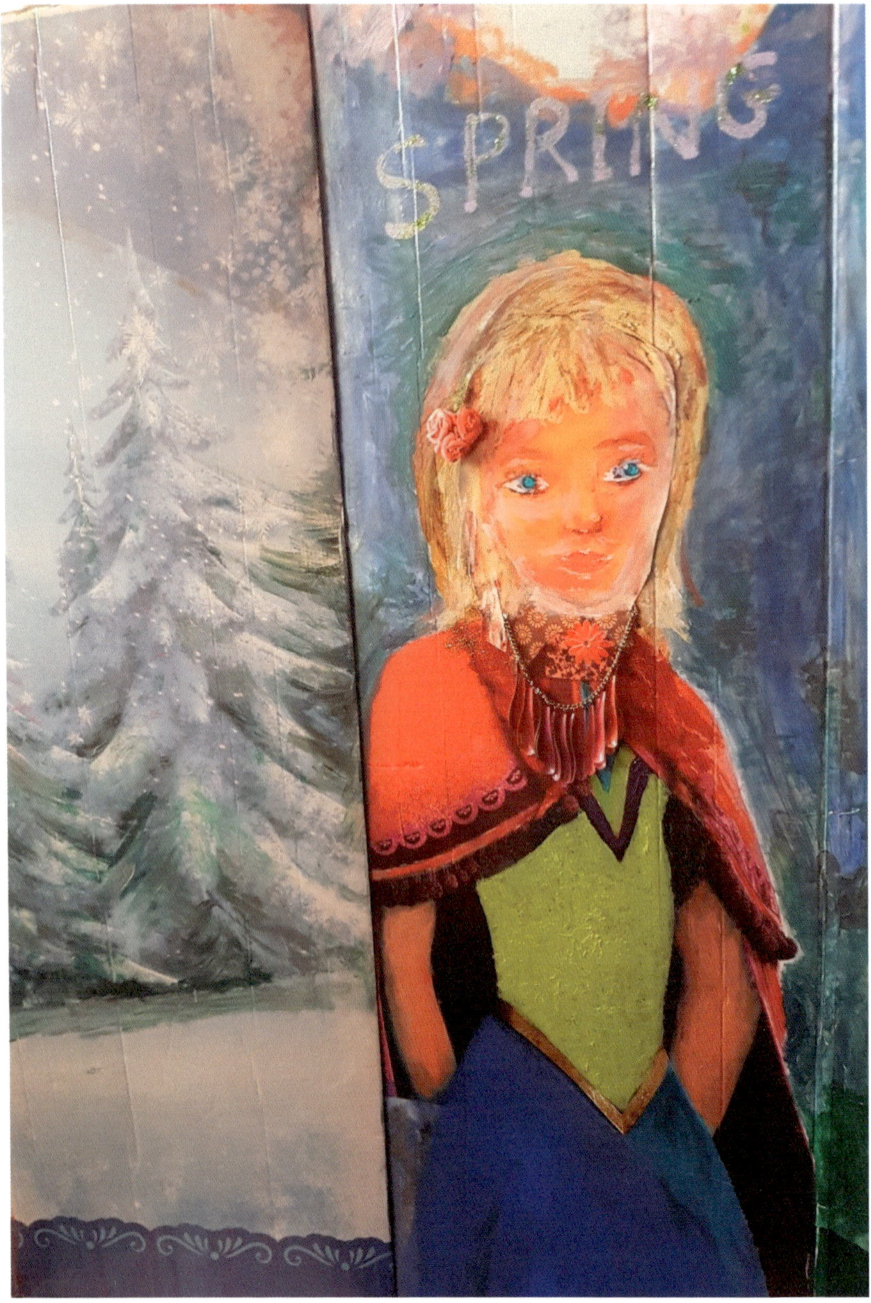
SPRING

SUMMER

Although the blues depicted above are pale, Summers also look great in cornflower blue. The pinks can be as warm as what I call Peppa pig pink as this summer wears on her necklace!

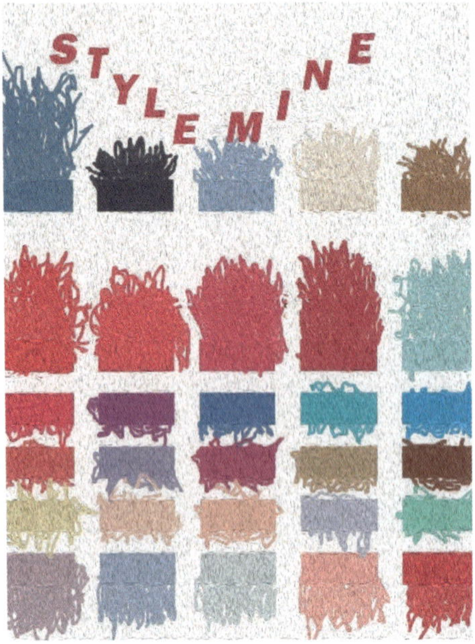
STYLEMINE

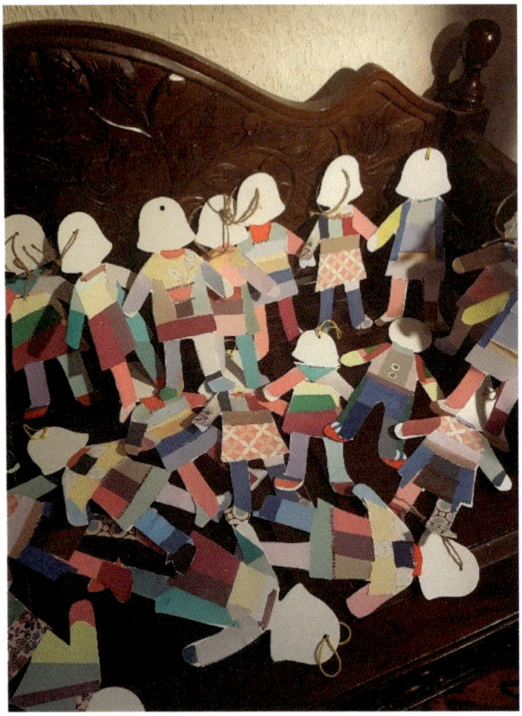

AUTUMN

Earthy Autumn, I could envisage a copper kettle heating by the hearth with some rosy apples in a basket!

WINTER

Stark contrasts of Winter light!

Cool defined colours.

18

Muted and vivid Seasons

Cool seasoned people Summer or Winter should find that silver compliments them best, rose gold is often an option.

Warm seasoned people Spring or Autumn will need to choose gold and copper coloured jewelry to compliment their colouring and clothing the best. As a rule (that can be adapted) the coolest and most muted season summer can sometimes need some care so as not to be diminished by either colour or intensity such as jewelry or style enhancing that is just a bit too overpowering (unless that's a look you're aiming for) which is quite reasonable, a look can always be vamped up with makeup! Seasonal colour analysis works subtly on summers, so to do more than bring out that glow doesn't really seem necessary and can detract. In the Summer when the sun is strongest or for a holiday it's a good idea to opt for a little bolder intensity in style and colour so that the sun doesn't wash you out, but there are many strong colours and variations to choose from, true red can work for all.

The other cool season Winter doesn't have so much risk of over powering if colours that are too warm are avoided and the seasonal colours are followed. This is because it is in the bold grouping. The colours that jump out at you should be icy ones straight from a winter scene bold and cold.

The warm season Spring has so many gorgeous salmon pinks. The colours have a lot of pigment and are so positively happy that they just spring out at you. For a more formal look, opting for navy is great. No matter which warm colour is worn they won't over power a true spring as its one of the bold seasons.

Autumn has more depth of tone than spring it can draw you in rather than spring to life, and that warm fuzzy feeling it provides can be comforting and earthy if desired. If a more formal image is required, the petrol blues in Autumn are magnificent as are the crimsons a warm a splash of bold and intense pigment is often a good option.

So, a golden rule for those in either muted or bold colour analysis grouping is that the bolds should not be diminished by faded colours, and the muted should not be over whelmed by overly strong colours.

Warm seasoned people will not be flattered by cool colours.

Cool seasoned people will not be enhanced by warm colours.

The varying degrees of warm and cool or bold and muted within the individual are key to determining how much of the warm or bold pigment they can accommodate.

How to develop an eye for colour

The actual process of instinctively categorizing a client's season is where I begin, its where we must defocus a little to really see the tones and intensity and just let whatever comes forward or recede be noted. Spend some time looking at the colour charts and paper dolls, it's all about absorbing this colour knowledge so you don't need to always refer to it. Once a feeling for it has developed it becomes a sense, and that is really what it is all about.

1. Does the client have warm or cold colouring?

First check the underside of the wrist do the veins have a green or blue hue? Green would indicate warm. This is how we look beneath the top surface of skin to see undertones.

2. Do their feature appear to have a harmony of intensity hair eyes skin all seem to be moderately blended in first tone and warmth, or do some features have something strong or contrasting, for instance bright blue eyes, or pale skin and dark hair? If they are blended, they will be either Autumn of Summer.

3. The general characteristics of a person's colouring mentioned here are fairly wide ranging within seasons. But there is another good way to categorize that is often correct once you've absorbed the rules of colour analysis – Which season do they resemble, if they were a work of art, a nature scene with all its splendid colours and contrasts?

4. Which seasonal colours would not suit, is a final check to be certain that the season assigned for a client is the correct one. Its easier to see this work in action, its unfailing and one of the reasons I am such a believer in this method of finding clothing harmony for many happy clients!

Shopping tips

One great tip that I learnt when I trained was once a season has been established, shop during that season for your various needs, because all the clothing stores will be aware of colour analysis and be using it abundantly with seasonal coloured items in various fashion ranges during the very season that will suit you best!

While you are still learning your season carry a reminder with you. I sell keyrings with fabric swatches seasonally matched, jewelry even makeup bags and purses. It makes it easier to refer to while you are learning your new amazing skill!

If you have muted seasonal colouring and are Summer or have greying hair and are looking for some more warmth in the colour of your clothing try a mix of neutral fabric with some autumn colour flecked through, marle is a good option as you will have lovely warm glow without being over powered. This is especially nice in winter knits just when we all need a bit of warming up. There are ways to adapt the rules to suit each person and occasion as long as the seasons are the foundation.

Remember if you are cool keep the warms further from your face, if warm keep the muted colours lower. If you are quite pale or muted keep the intense shades from your face and if you have a strong vibrancy keep the more faded colours for skirts or trousers.

I will share with you some more tips that you can absorb visually and after that show you some of the clients that I've recently styled as they demonstrate the seasons really well.

STYLEMINE

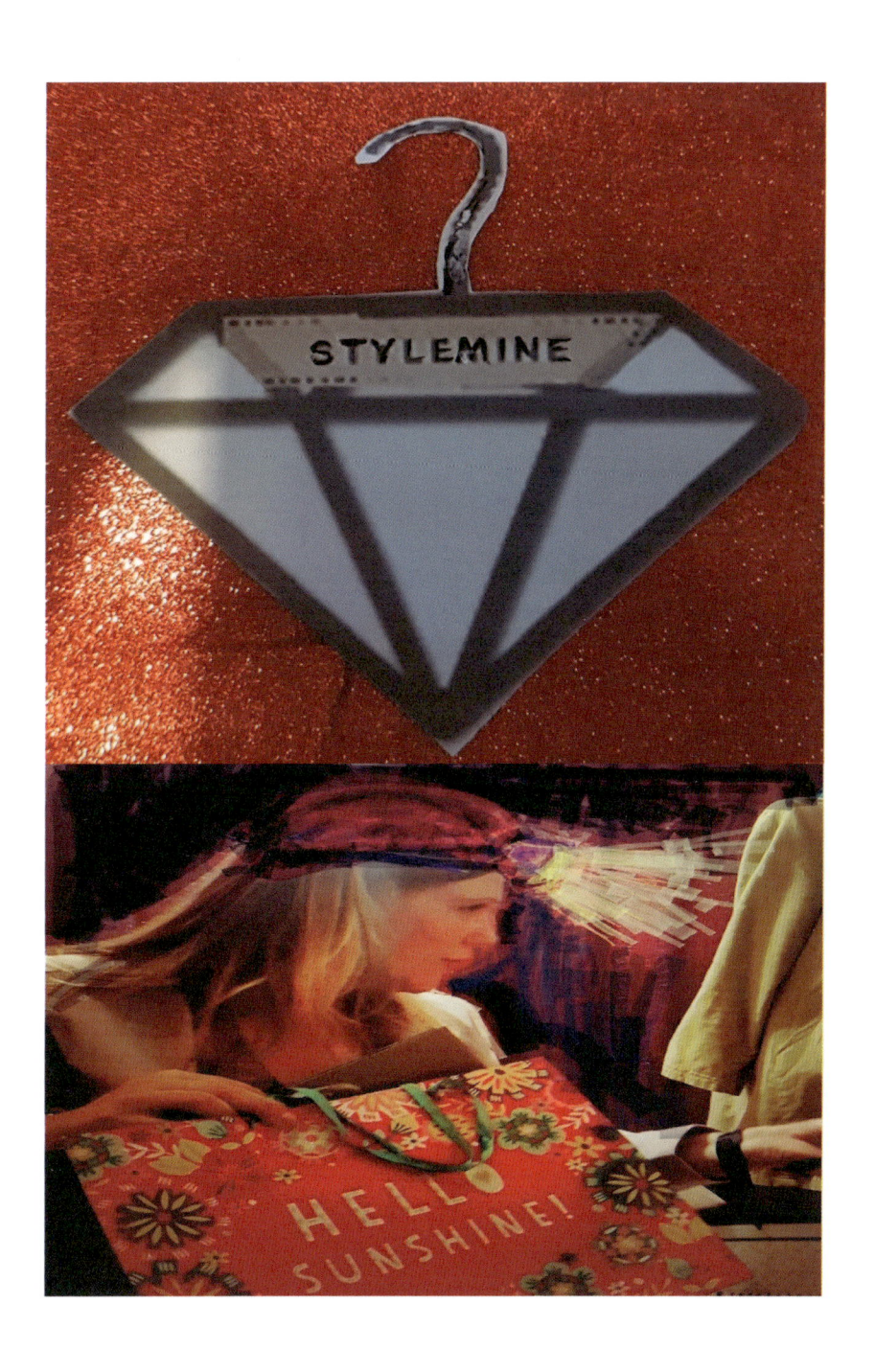

Summer top is quite visually different from Spring, cool and not strongly pigmented it feels like summer!

Winter feels icy and Autumn feels warm!

Both summers as you can see the hair and skin tone blend together with little contrasting intensity.

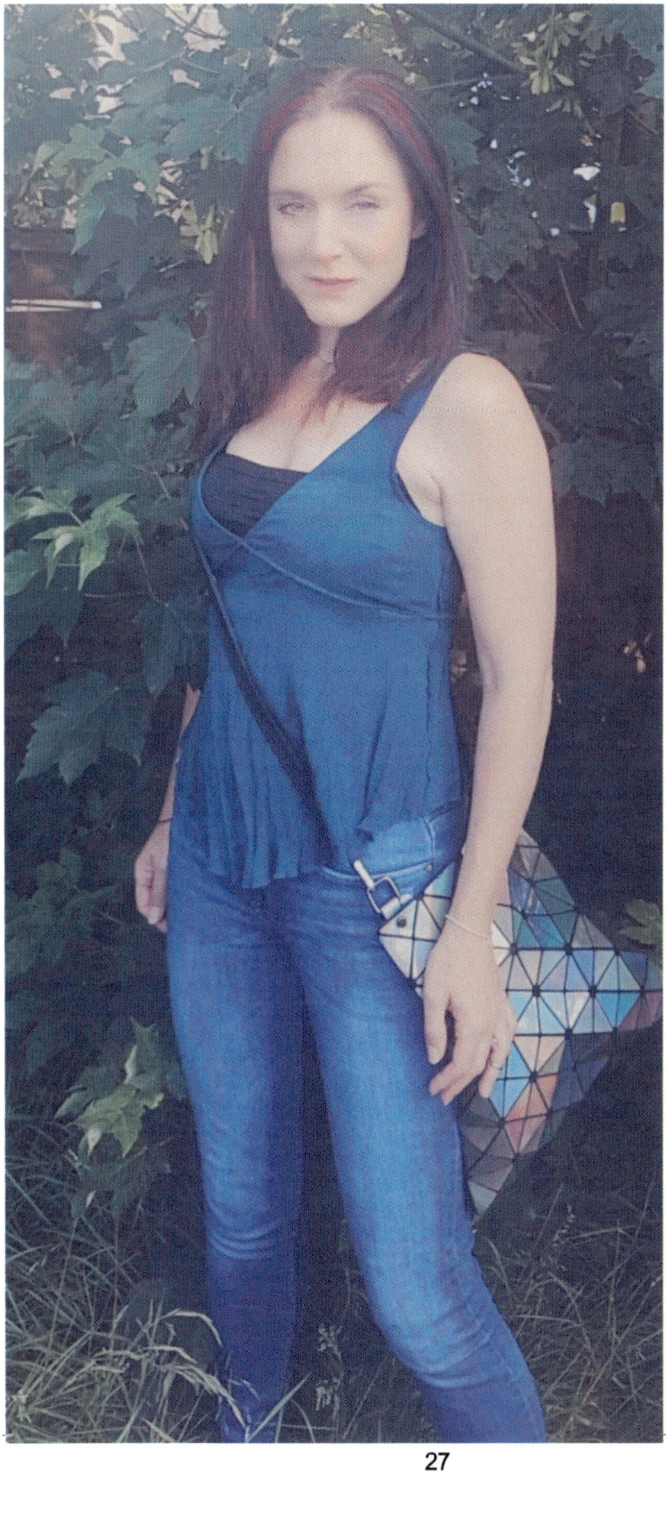

My client on the previous page depicts a cool and contrasting Winter.

The high contrast between hair and skin is very noticeable. My clients skin is fair and translucent, and her dark hair provides an eye-catching distinction between the two.

See how the silver bag effortlessly connects the rest of the cool tones and brings them together.

The red streaks in her hair don't change the season to a warmer one, as they don't override the rest of her colouring and are of a cooler burgundy red rather than a chestnut.

My client is a cool Winter!

My very seasonal Christmas Stylmemine cabin selling lots of glitzy coordinating seasonal accessories and offering seasonal colour analysis! I hope you have learnt something practical about the tricks of the colour analysis trade and are ready to take the plunge and see how it works for you! If you would like some more assistance my website is -
www.stylemine.co.uk
Once you've inwardly absorbed the colour blend of each season it becomes a lot easier and visualization of the colour collections I've put together can help with that.

    Good luck on your journeys

        Samantha Louise

Printed in Great Britain
by Amazon